Bass Fitness · An Exercising Handbook

By Josquin des Pres

Josquin des Pres is a French-American bass player who has appeared (... ... ... albums and CDs both as a studio musician and sideman.

Over the past few decades, he has shared credits with some of the premier musicians of our time: Alex Acuna, Steve Lukather, Jerry Goodman, David Garibaldi, Jack Johnson, Bunny Brunel, Stanley Clarke, Steve Bailey, Victor Wooten, John Jorgensen, Jerry Donahue, Charlie Daniels, Peter Frampton, The Gipsy Kings, Jeff Porcaro, Billy Sheehan, and many more.

Josquin is also a prolific songwriter, composer, and producer. He has written over a dozen songs with legendary lyricist Bernie Taupin (of Elton John fame), produced close to a hundred albums, and composes music for dozens of TV networks.

Also available:

Bass Fitness – Ultimate Woodshedding App!
Now you can play all the Bass Fitness exercises in this book along with demo tracks or a metronome, set tempos, loop, and record yourself for more enhanced practice on 4-, 5-, and 6-string bass.

For iPhone, iPad, and iPod Touch.

ISBN 978-0-7935-0248-6

7777 W. Bluemound Rd. P.O. Box 13819 Milwaukee, WI 53213

In Australia Contact:
Hal Leonard Australia Pty. Ltd.
4 Lentara Court
Cheltenham, Victoria, 3192 Australia
Email: ausadmin@halleonard.com.au

Visit Hal Leonard Online at
www.halleonard.com

The purpose of this book is to provide the aspiring bass player with a wide variety of finger exercises indispensable to anyone wanting to develop the technique necessary to succeed in today's music scene. It can also play a very important role in a bass player's daily practicing program.

This book is dedicated to the memory of my father, **Francois Turenne des Pres** (May 4, 1907 / November 29, 1990) for his lifelong support and infinite inspiration, and **David Paul Schuchman,** (November 2, 1960 / September 1, 1989). His encouragement and help gave me the initial force in writing it.

Josquin des Pres

Contents

These exercises are designed to help increase your speed, improve your dexterity, develop accuracy and promote finger independence.

Even though all the tablature and finger combinations apply to the left hand, they will also work your right hand as some of them require swift and precise right hand moves.

The numbers on the tablatures indicate both frets and fingers:

Number 1 indicates the index finger as well as fret 1.

Number 2 indicates the middle finger as well as fret 2.

Number 3 indicates the ring finger as well as fret 3.

Number 4 indicates the little finger as well as fret 4.

Practice daily, playing each exercise **for at least 15 minutes** before moving on to the next one.

Play each exercise up and down, then move up chromatically in half steps (a half step equals one fret). Starting at fret 1 up to the 12th fret and back down.

Always use a metronome, playing 8th notes (2 notes per metronome click). Start at the **slowest indicated speed, concentrate on your sound,** then gradually speed up.

When crossing over strings be as precise as possible by watching alternatively your left and right hand.

Part A

Exercises with all 4 fingers moving across the fingerboard

♩ = 60/180

1
UP

DOWN

2
UP

DOWN

3
UP

DOWN

4
UP

DOWN

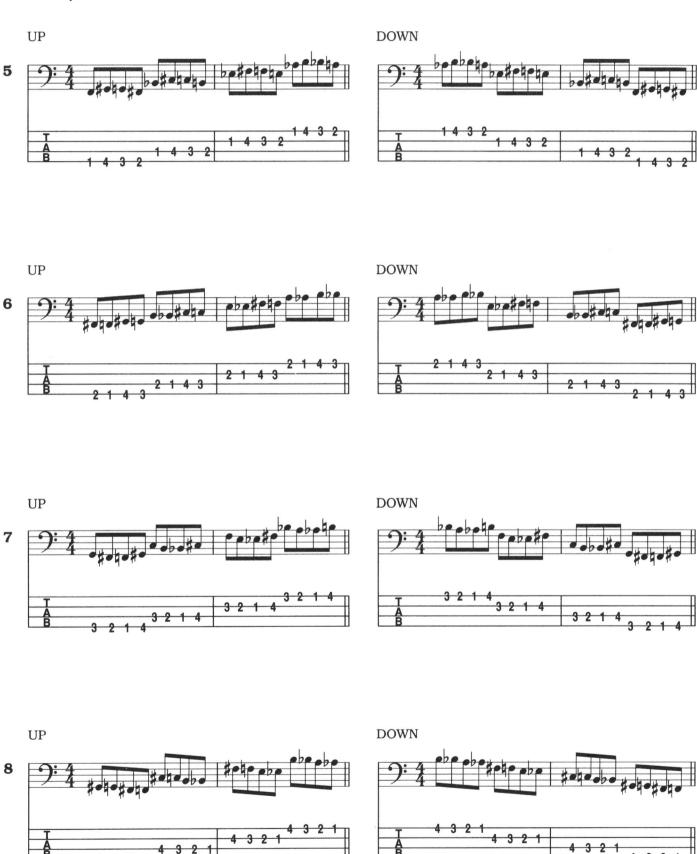

♩ = 60/180

UP
                                                  DOWN

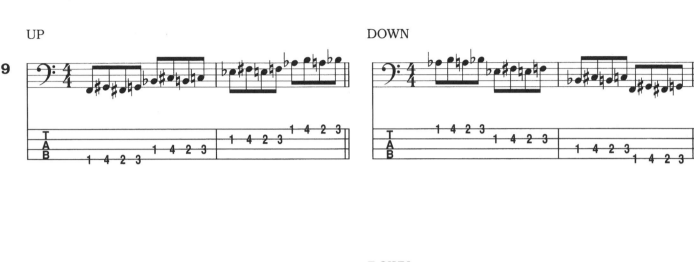

UP   DOWN

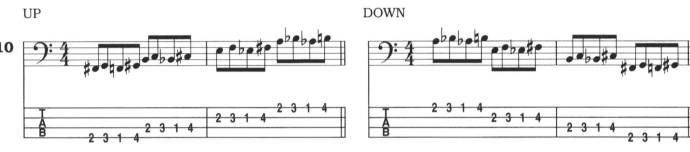

UP   DOWN

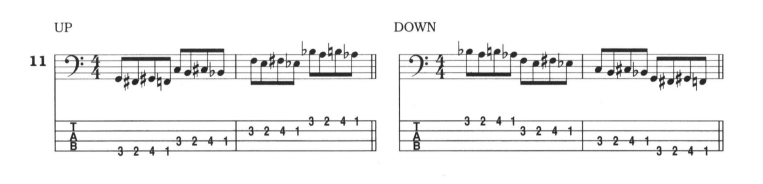

UP   DOWN

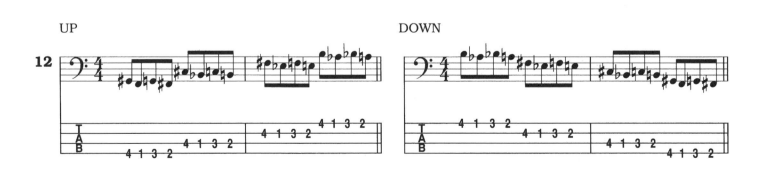

Part B

Exercises with 1 finger remaining in the same position and 3 moving across the fingerboard

♩ = 60/180

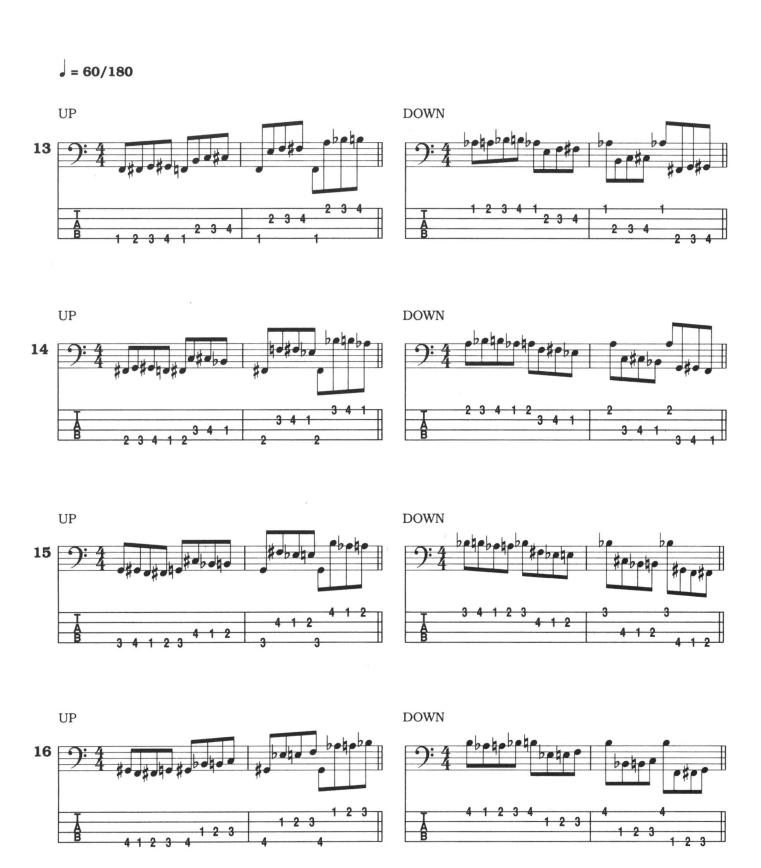

♩ = 60/180

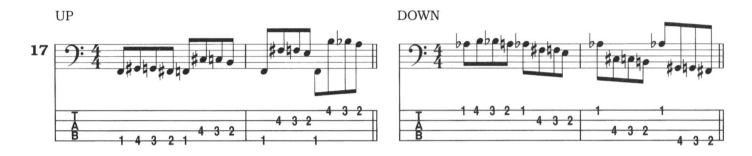

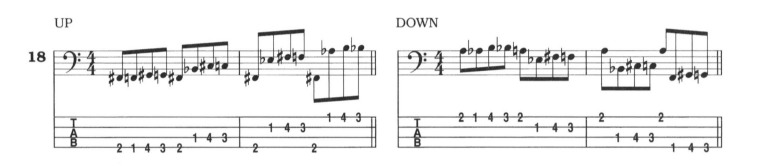

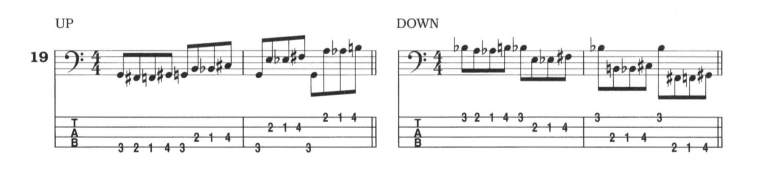

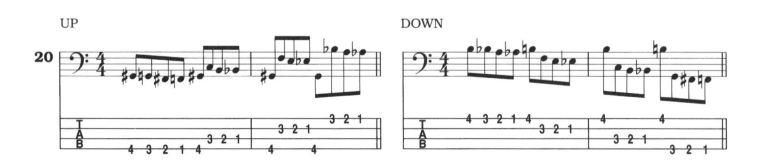

♩ = 60/180

UP

21

DOWN

UP

22

DOWN

UP

23

DOWN
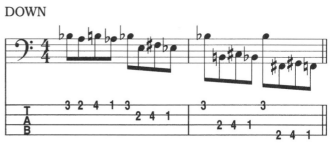

UP

24

DOWN

Part C

Exercises with 2 fingers remaining in the same position and 2 moving across the fingerboard

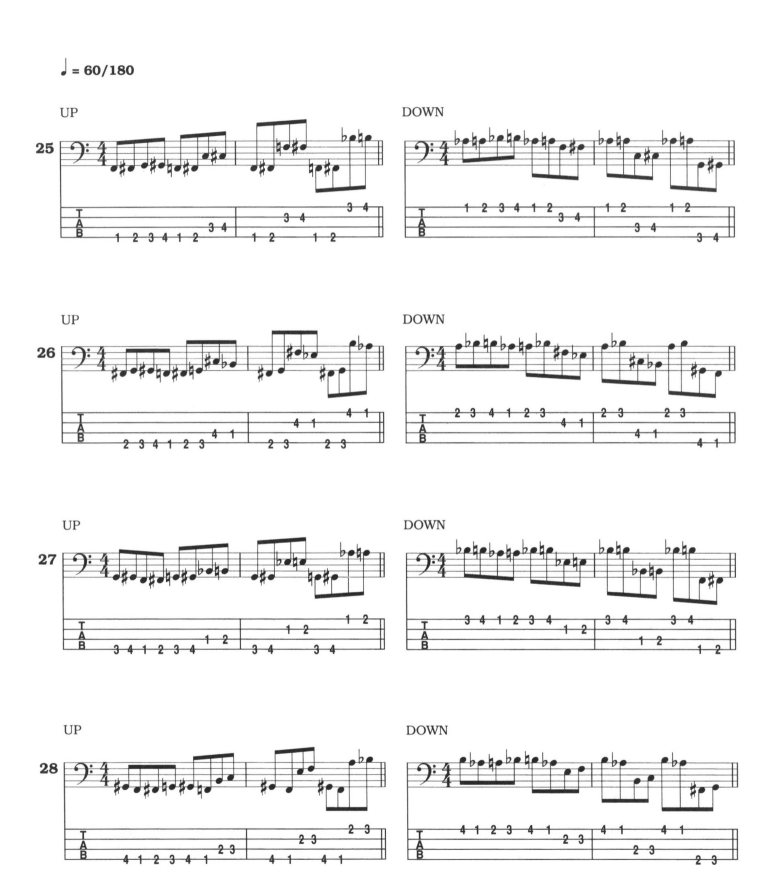

♩ = 60/180

UP

29

DOWN

UP

30

DOWN

UP

31

DOWN

UP

32

DOWN

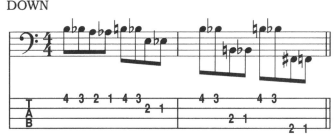

♩ = 60/180

UP

33

DOWN

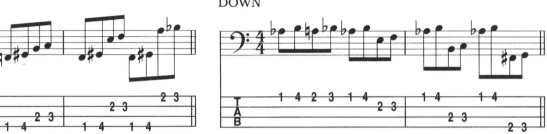

UP

34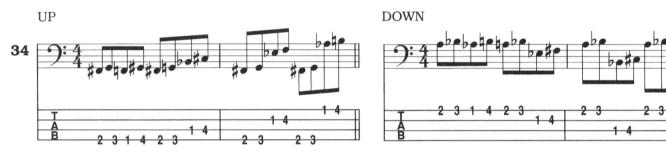

DOWN

UP

35

DOWN

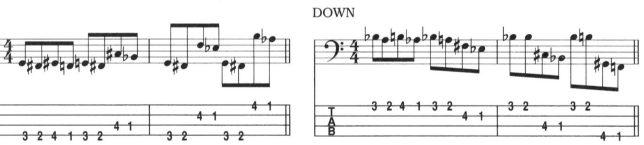

UP

36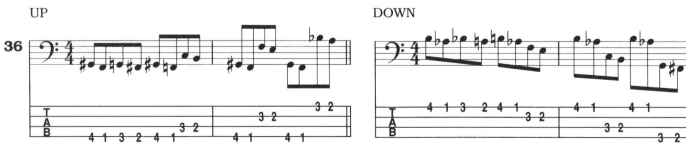

DOWN

Part D

Exercises with 3 fingers remaining in the same position and 1 moving across the fingerboard

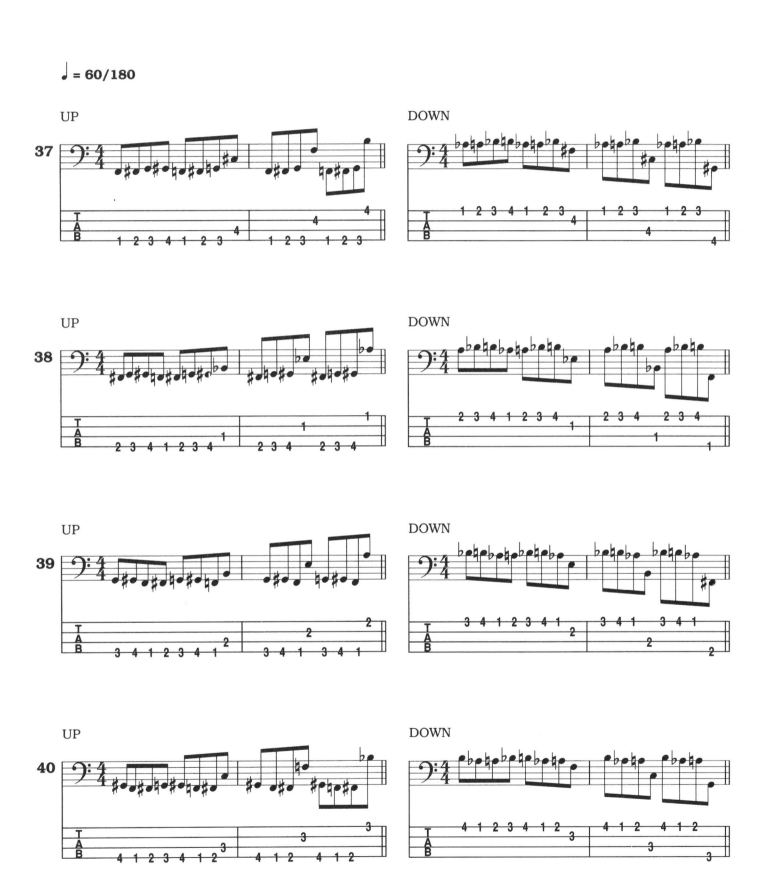

♩ = 60/180

UP

DOWN

41

UP

DOWN

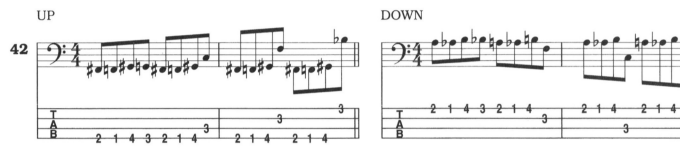

42

UP

DOWN

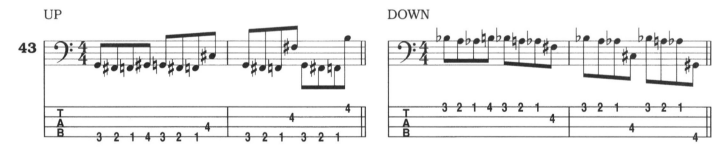

43

UP

DOWN

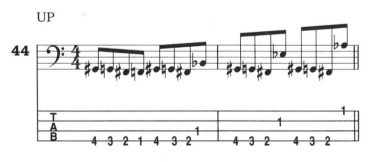

44

♩ = 60/180

UP

45

DOWN

UP

46

DOWN

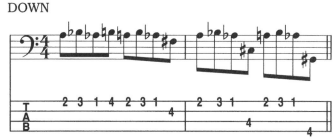

UP

47

DOWN

UP

48

DOWN

Part A

Variations of the exercises contained in Section 1

♩ = 60/180

UP

DOWN

49

UP

DOWN

50

UP

DOWN

51

UP

DOWN

52

♩ = 60/180

UP

DOWN

UP

DOWN

UP

DOWN

UP

DOWN

♩ = 60/180

UP

DOWN

UP

DOWN

UP

DOWN

UP

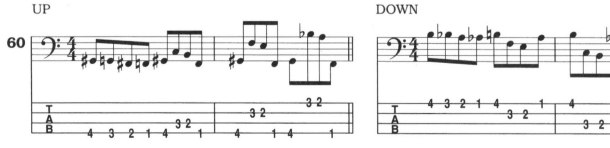

DOWN

Part A

*Exercises alternating direction, with all 4 fingers
moving across the fingerboard*

♩ = 60/180

61

UP

DOWN

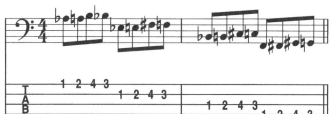

62

UP

DOWN

63

UP

DOWN

64

UP

DOWN

Part B

Exercises alternating direction, with 1 finger remaining in the same position and 3 moving across the fingerboard

 = 60/180

UP

DOWN

UP

DOWN

UP

DOWN
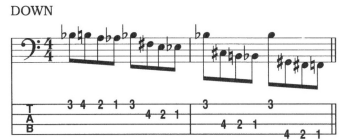

UP

DOWN
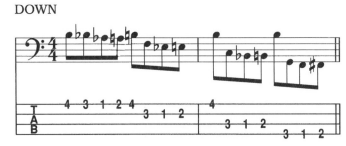

Part C

*Exercises alternating direction, with 2 fingers remaining
in the same position and 2 moving across the fingerboard*

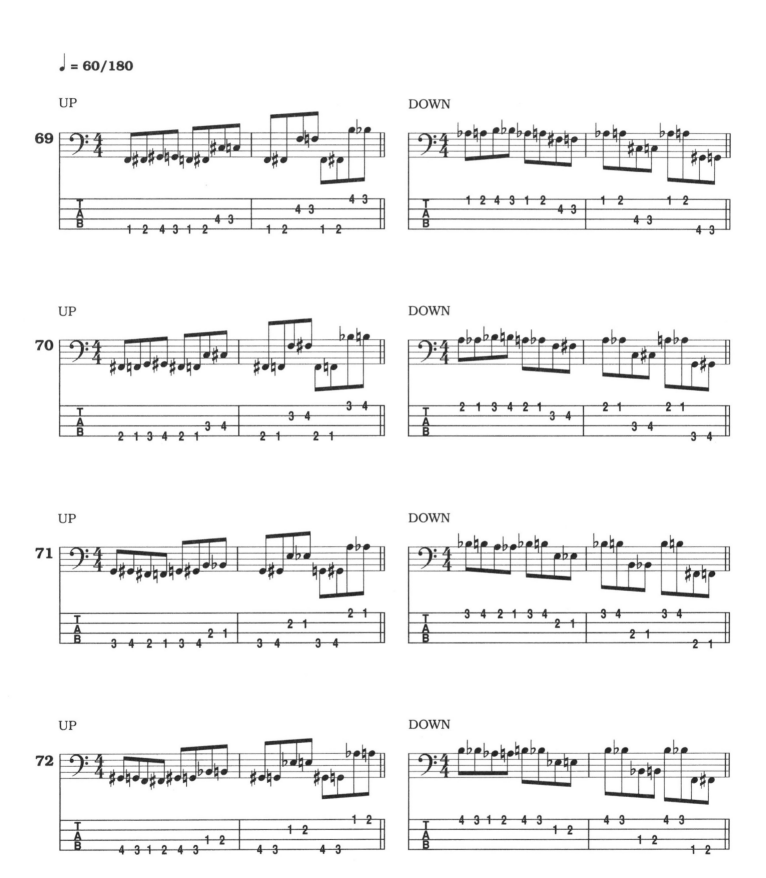

Part D

*Exercises alternating direction, with 3 fingers remaining in the
same position and 1 moving across the fingerboard*

♩ = 60/180

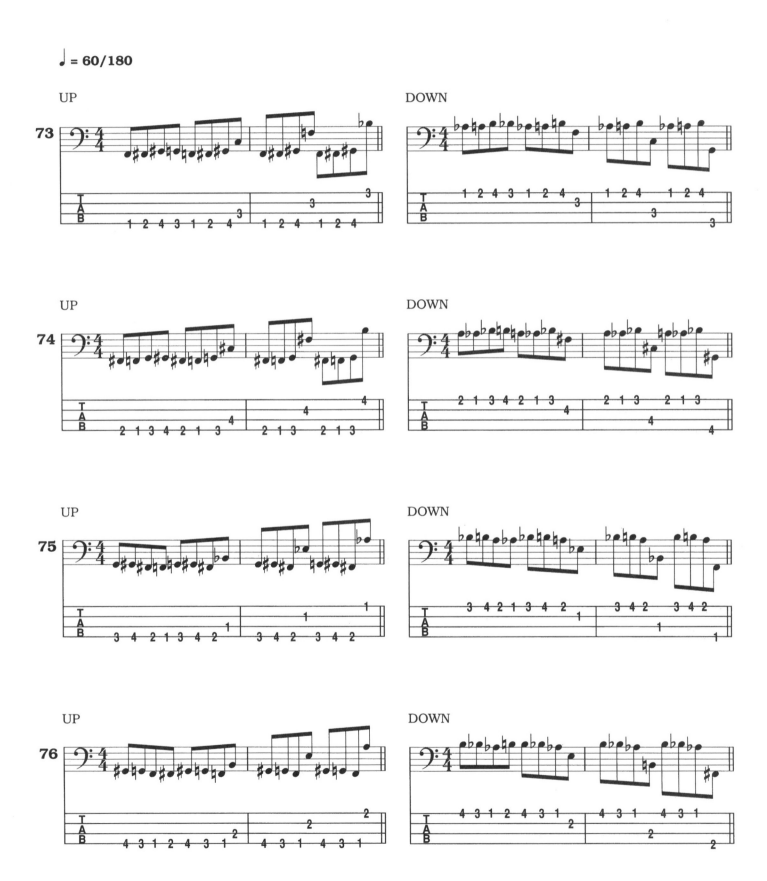

SECTION FOUR

Variations of the exercises contained in Section 3

 = **60/180**

UP  DOWN

77

UP  DOWN

78

UP  DOWN

79

UP  DOWN

80

♩ = 60/180

UP

DOWN

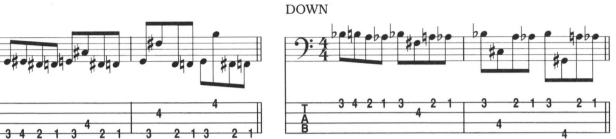

81

UP

DOWN

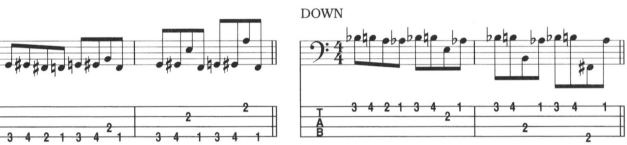

82

UP

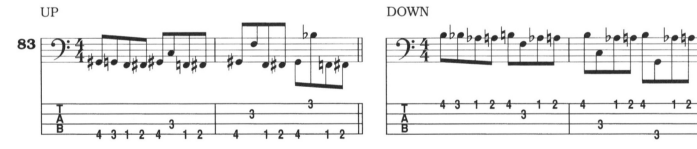

DOWN

83

UP

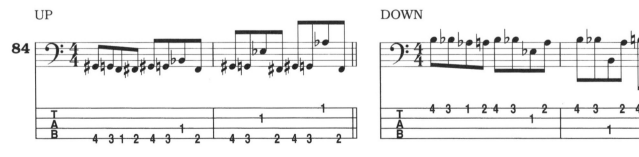

DOWN

84

♩ = 60/180

UP   DOWN

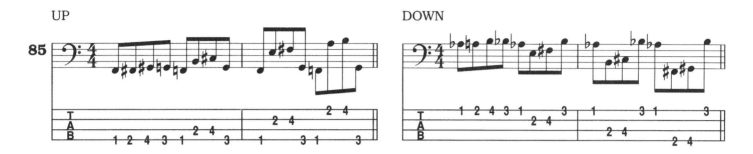

UP   DOWN

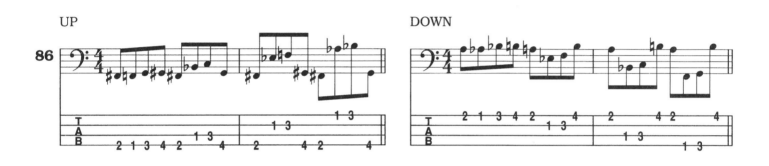

UP   DOWN

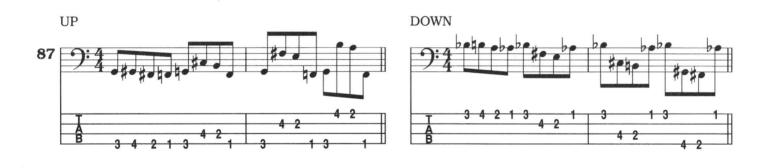

UP   DOWN

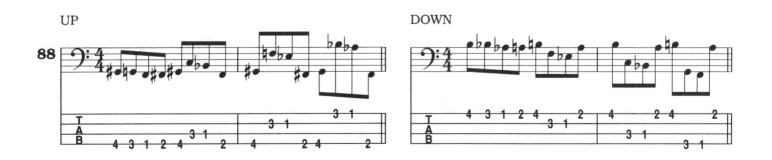

Part A

Exercises for skipping frets, with all 4 fingers moving across the fingerboard

SECTION FIVE

 = 60/180

UP   DOWN

89

UP   DOWN

90

UP   DOWN

91

UP   DOWN

92

Part B

Exercises for skipping frets, with 1 finger remaining
in the same position and 3 moving across the fingerboard

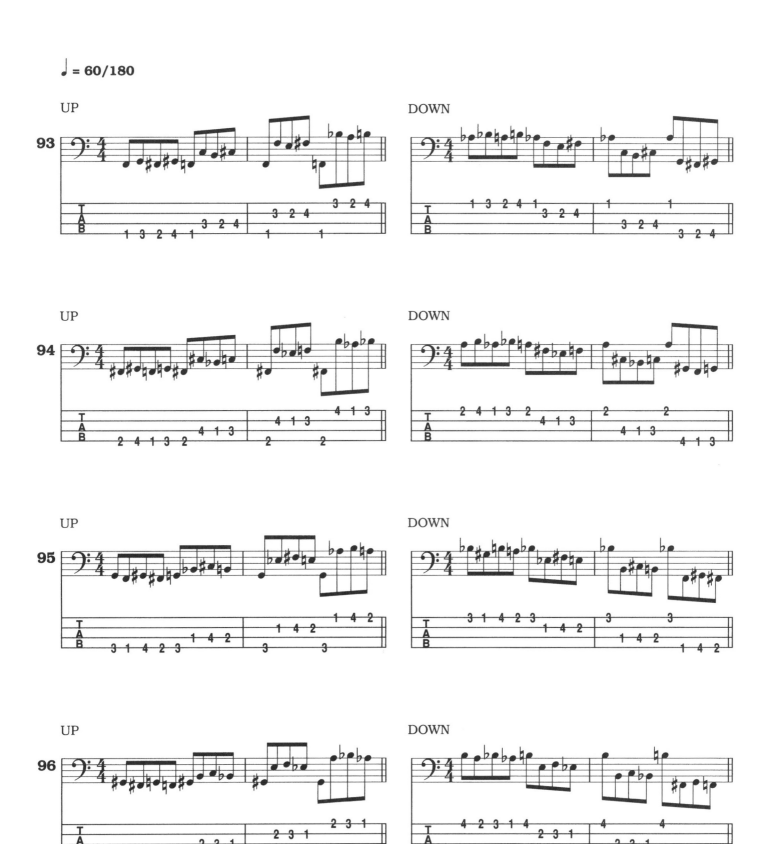

Part C

*Exercises for skipping frets, with 2 fingers remaining
in the same position and 2 moving across the fingerboard*

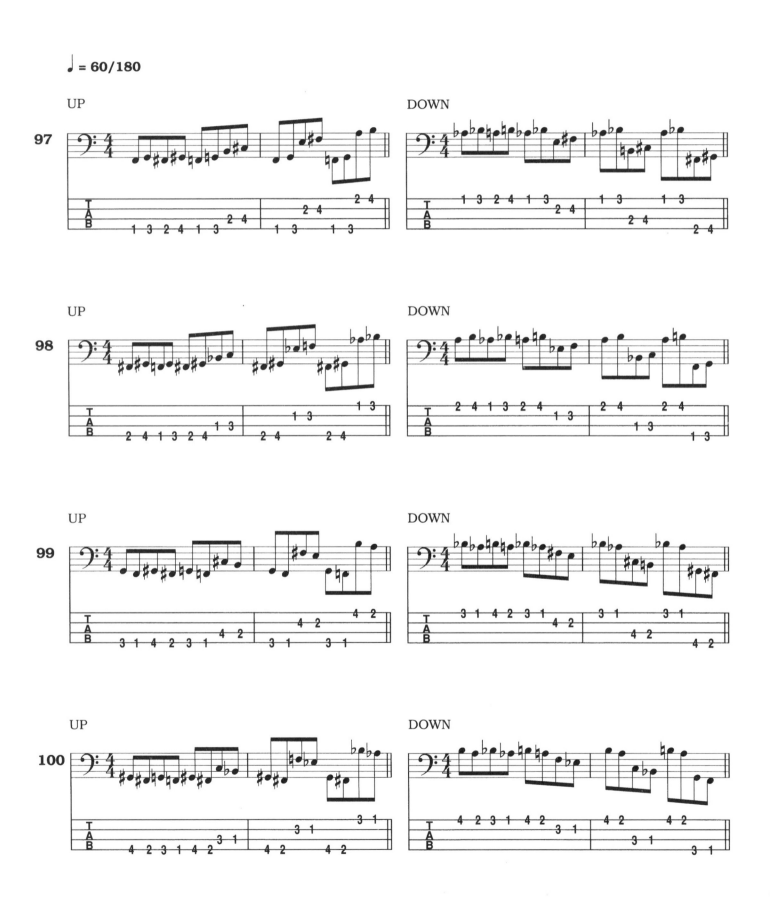

Part D

Exercises for skipping frets, with 3 fingers remaining in the same position and 1 moving across the fingerboard

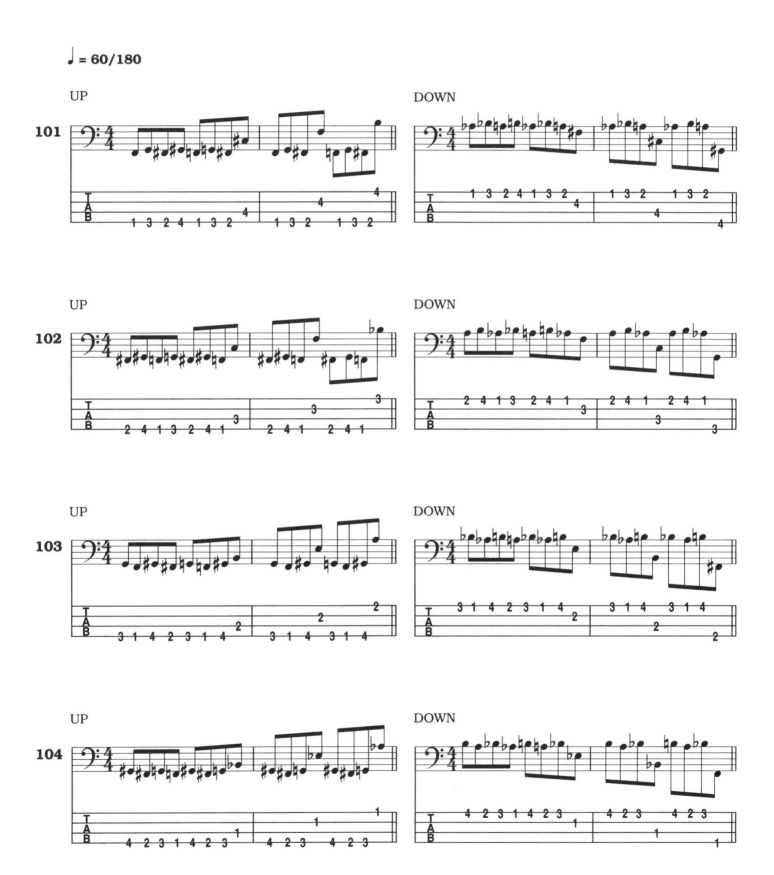

Part A

Exercises for skipping frets, alternating direction,
with all 4 fingers moving across the fingerboard

 = 60/180

UP   DOWN

105

UP   DOWN

106

UP   DOWN

107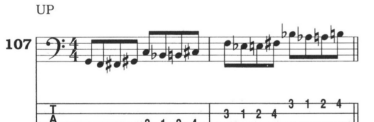

UP   DOWN

108

Part B

Exercises for skipping frets, alternating direction, with 1 finger remaining in the same position and 3 moving across the fingerboard

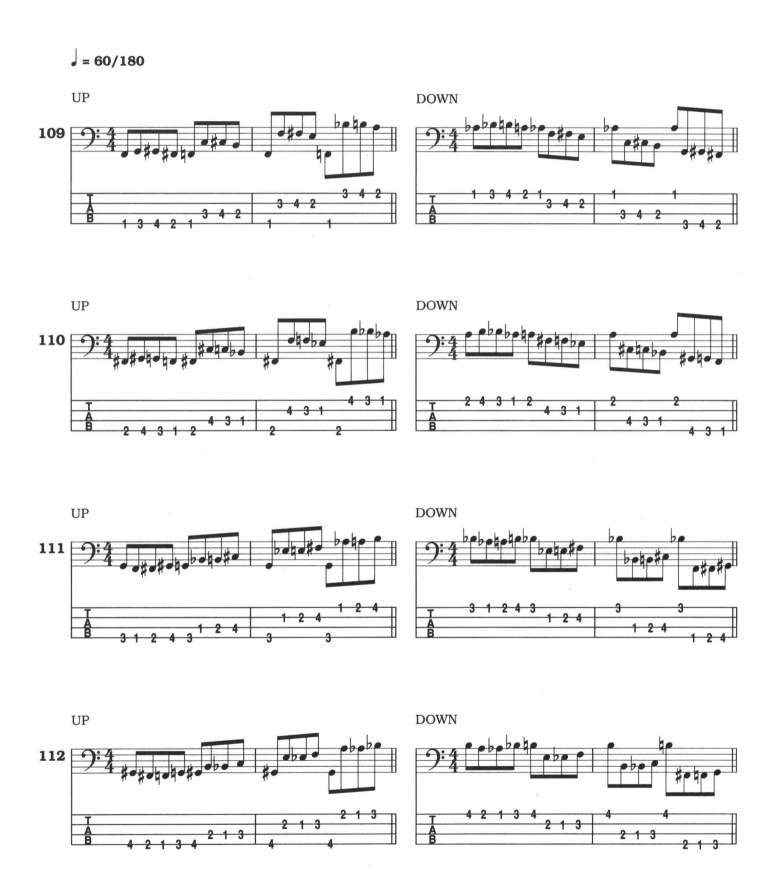

Part C

Exercises for skipping frets, alternating direction, with 2 fingers
remaining in the same position and 2 moving across the fingerboard

Part D

Exercises for skipping frets, alternating direction, with 3 fingers
remaining in the same position and 1 moving across the fingerboard

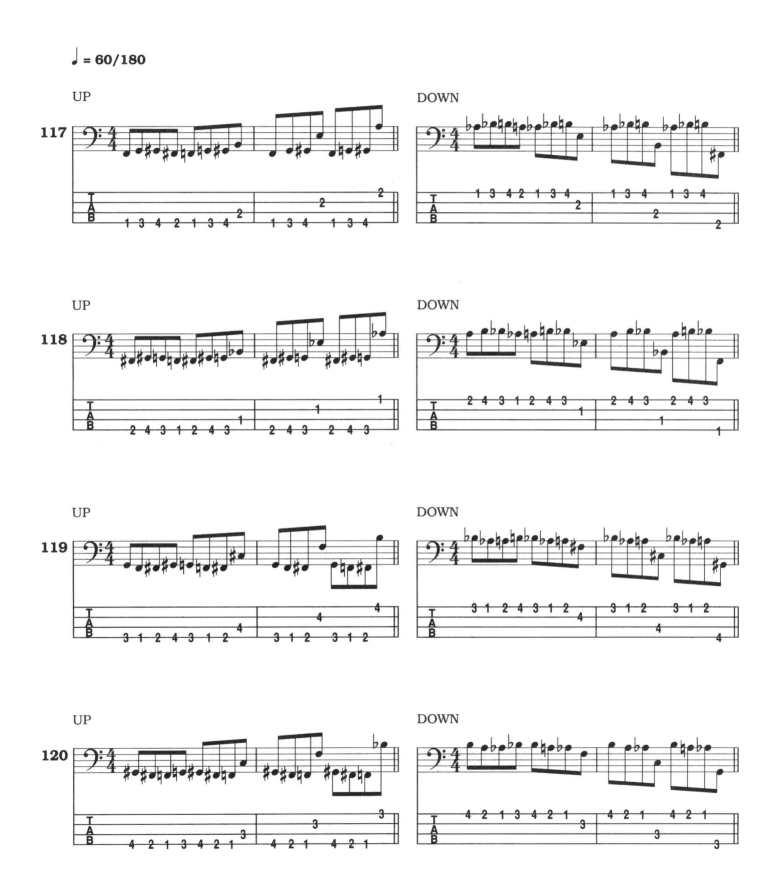

Part A

Exercises for moving between strings

 = 60/180

121 UP  DOWN

122 UP  DOWN

123 UP  DOWN

124 UP  DOWN

UP

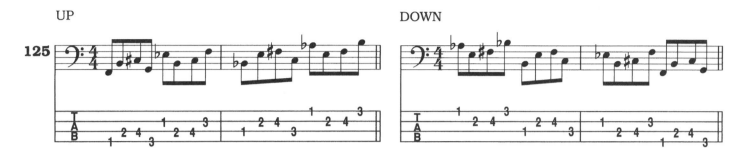

UP

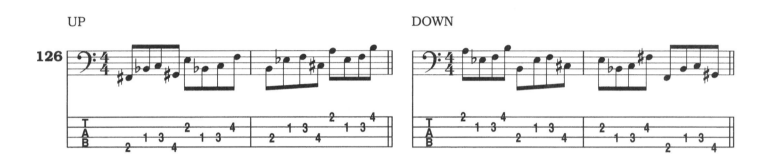

UP

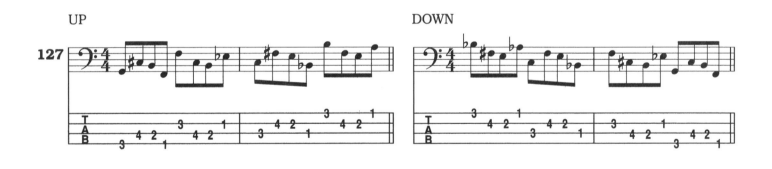

UP

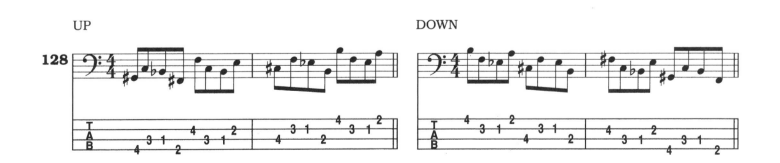

Part B

Exercises for skipping strings

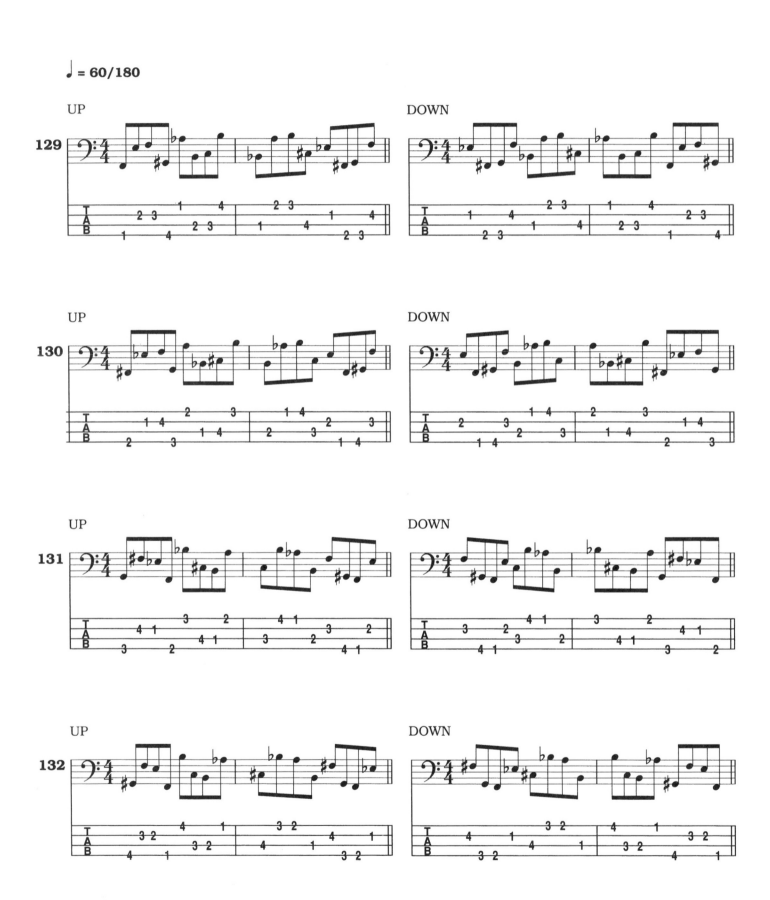

♩ = 60/180

UP   DOWN

133
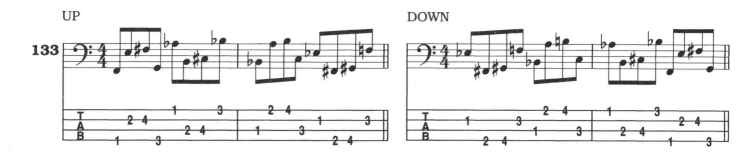

UP   DOWN

134
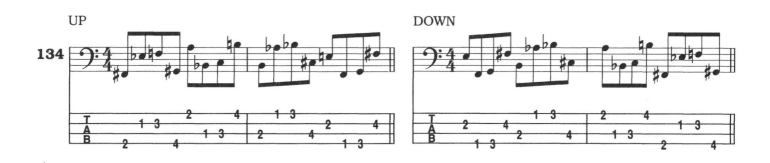

UP   DOWN

135
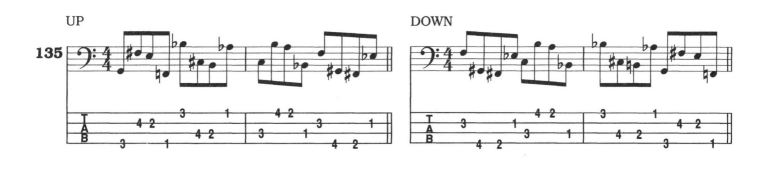

UP   DOWN

136
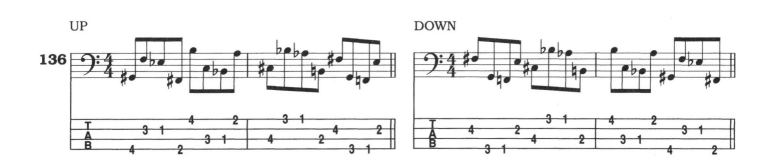

Part A

Exercises for moving back and forth between strings

UP   DOWN

137

UP   DOWN

138

UP   DOWN

139

UP   DOWN

140

Part B

Exercises for moving back and forth between strings, alternating direction

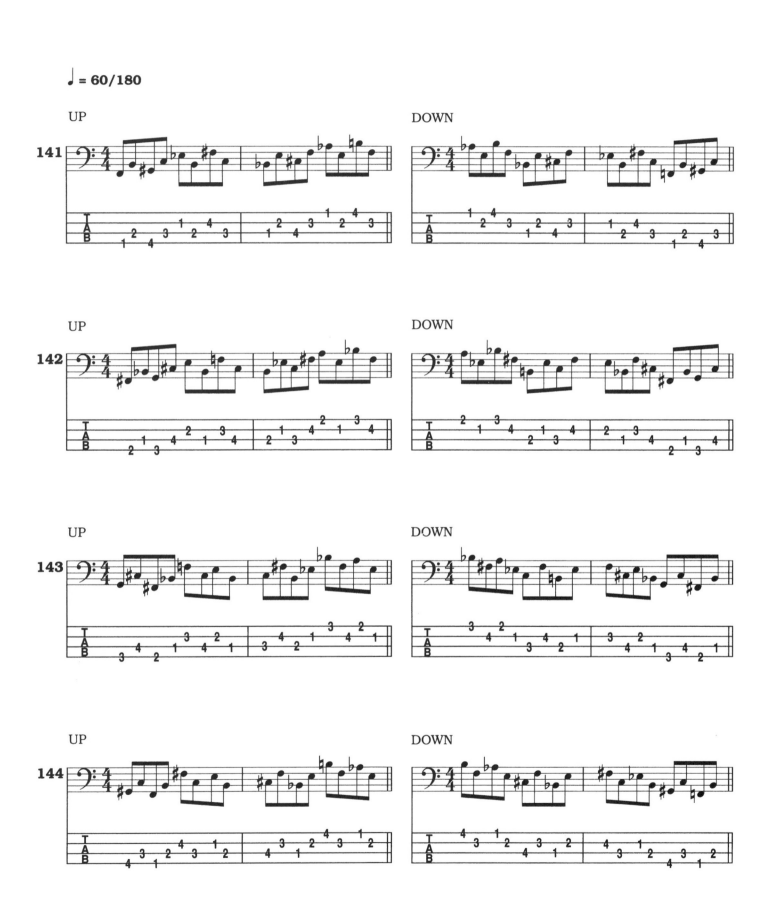

Part C

Exercises for skipping back and forth between strings

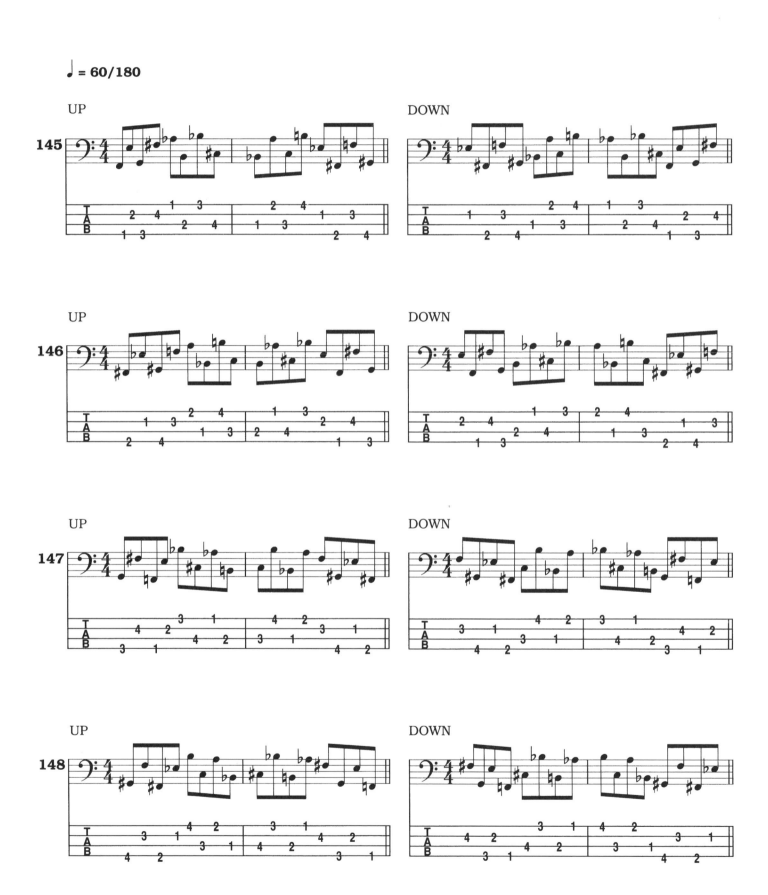

Part D

Exercises for skipping back and forth between strings alternating direction

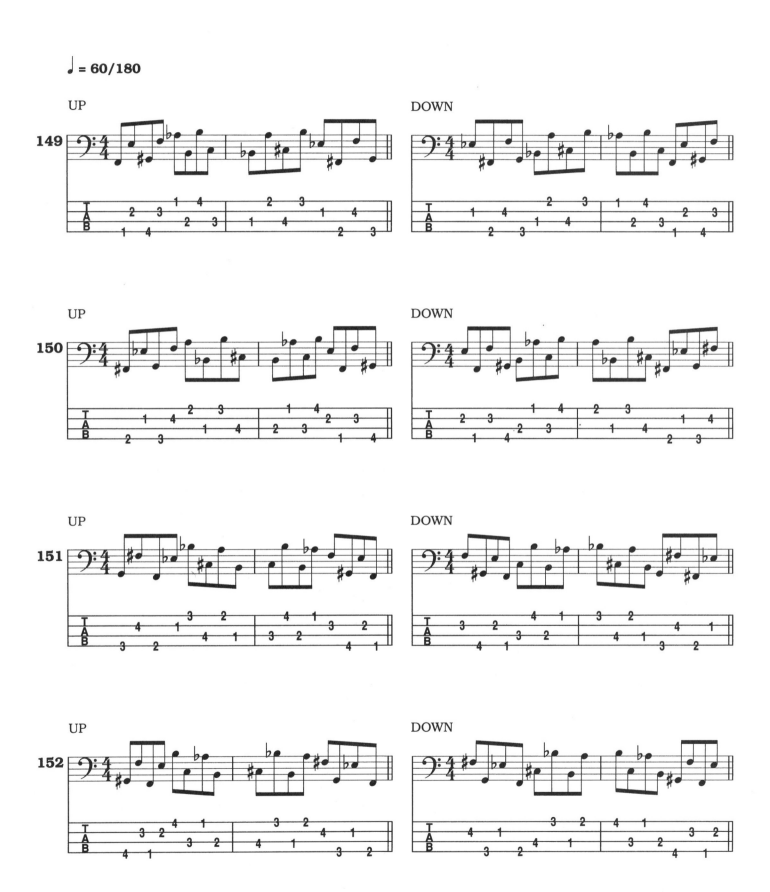

Part A

*Finger independence exercises centered
around finger #1 (upward motion)*

♩ = 60/180

UP

DOWN

UP

DOWN

♩ = 60/180

UP

155

DOWN

UP

156

DOWN

♩ = 60/180

UP

157

DOWN

UP

158

DOWN

♩ = 60/180

UP

159

DOWN

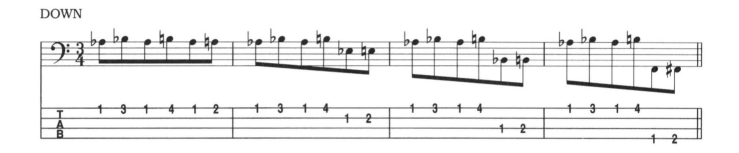

UP

160

DOWN

♩ = 60/180

UP

DOWN

UP

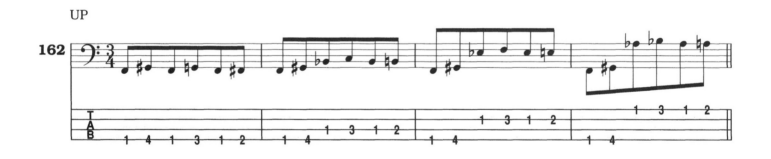

DOWN

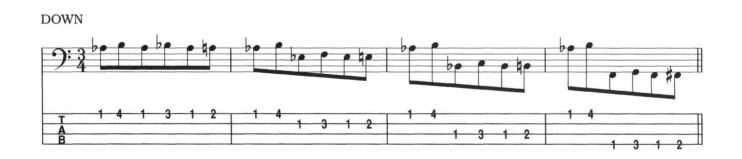

♩ = 60/180

UP

DOWN

UP

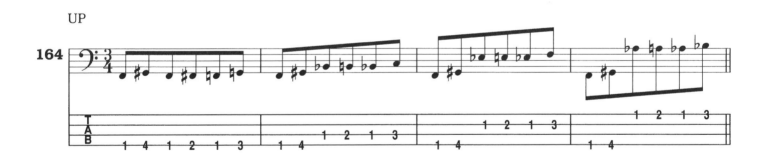

DOWN

Part B

Finger independence exercises centered around finger #1 (downward motion)

UP

DOWN

UP

DOWN

♩ = 60/180

UP

DOWN

UP

DOWN

♩ = 60/180

UP

DOWN

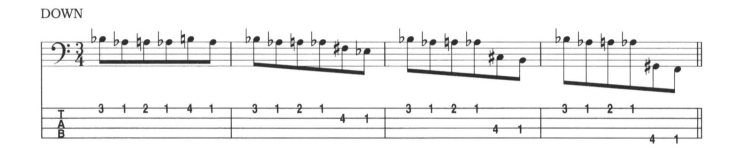

UP

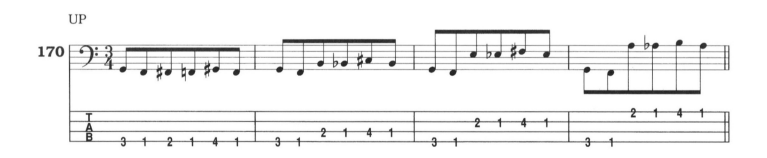

DOWN

♩ = 60/180

UP

DOWN

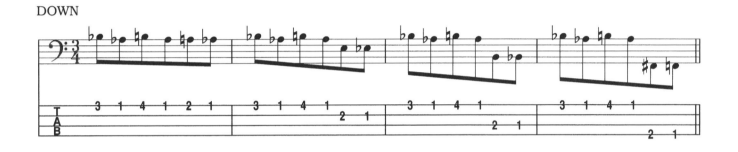

UP

DOWN

♩ = 60/180

UP

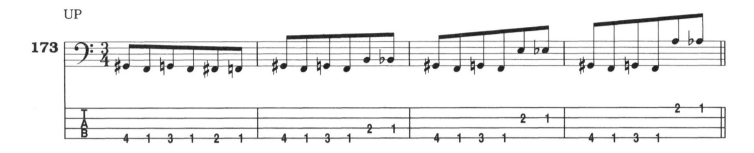

DOWN

UP

DOWN

♩ = 60/180

UP

DOWN

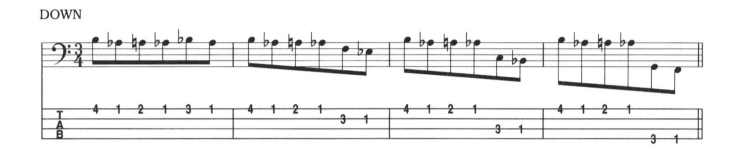

UP

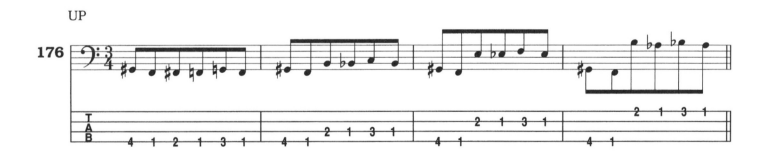

DOWN

Part A

Finger independence exercises centered around finger #4 (upward motion)

♩ = 60/180

UP

DOWN

UP

DOWN

♩ = 60/180

UP

179

DOWN

UP

180

DOWN

♩ = 60/180

UP

181

DOWN

UP

182

DOWN

$\quad$ = 60/180

UP

183

DOWN

UP

184

DOWN

♩ = 60/180

UP

DOWN

UP

DOWN

♩ = 60/180

UP

DOWN

UP

DOWN

Part B

Finger independence exercises centered around finger #4 (downward motion)

♩ = 60/180

UP

189

DOWN

UP

190

DOWN

♩ = 60/180

UP

DOWN

UP

DOWN

♩ = 60/180

UP

DOWN

UP

DOWN

♩ = 60/180

UP

195

DOWN

UP

196

DOWN

♩ = 60/180

UP

DOWN

UP

DOWN

♩ = 60/180

UP

199

DOWN

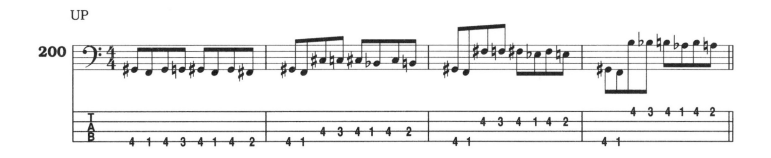

UP

200

DOWN

Part A

Exercises with all 4 fingers moving across the fingerboard

♩ = 60/180

UP

201

DOWN

UP

202

DOWN

♩ = 60/180

UP

203

DOWN

UP

204

DOWN

Part B

Variations of the exercises contained in Part A

♩ = 60/180

UP

205

DOWN

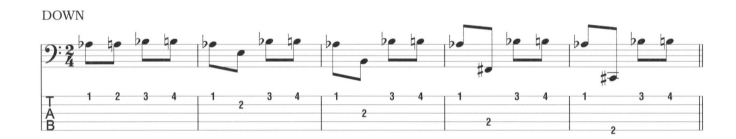

UP

206

♩ = 60/180

UP

DOWN

UP

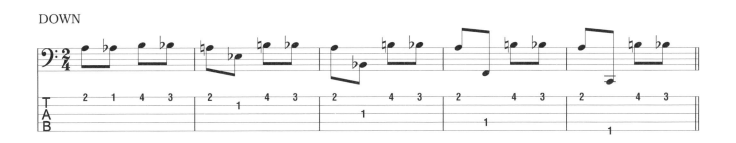

DOWN

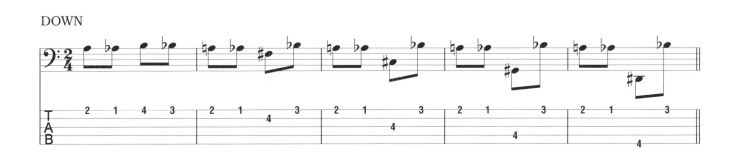

Part C

Exercises alternating direction, with all 4 fingers moving across the fingerboard

♩ = 60/180

UP

209

DOWN

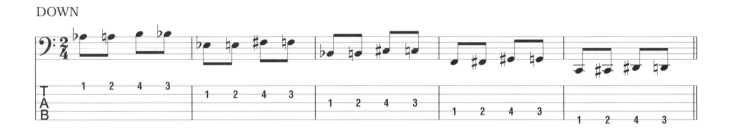

UP

210

DOWN

UP

211

DOWN

UP

212

DOWN

Part D

Variations of the exercises contained in Part C

♩ = 60/180

UP

DOWN

UP

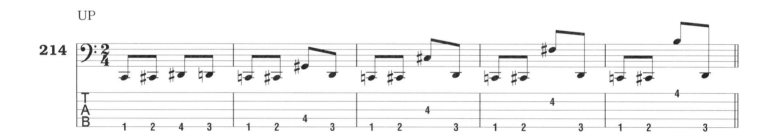

DOWN

UP

DOWN

UP

DOWN

Part E

Exercises for skipping frets, with all 4 fingers moving across the fingerboard

♩ = 60/180

UP

217

DOWN

UP

218

DOWN

UP

DOWN

UP

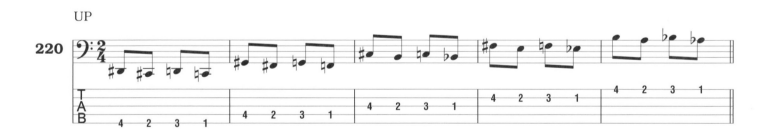

DOWN

Part F

Exercises for skipping frets, alternating direction, with all 4 fingers moving across the fingerboard

♩ = 60/180

UP

DOWN

UP

DOWN

UP

223

DOWN
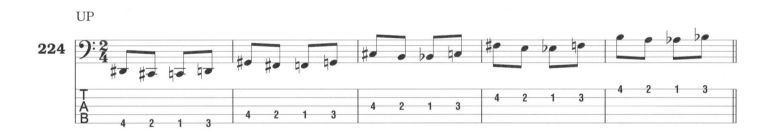

UP

224

DOWN

Part A

Exercises for moving between strings

♩ = 60/180

UP

225

DOWN

UP

226

DOWN

♩ = 60/180

UP

DOWN

UP

DOWN

Part B

Exercises for moving back and forth between strings

♩ = 60/180

UP

229

DOWN

UP

230

DOWN

♩ = 60/180

UP

DOWN

UP

DOWN

Part C

Finger independence exercises centered around finger #1 (upward motion)

♩ = 60/180

UP

233

DOWN

UP

234

DOWN

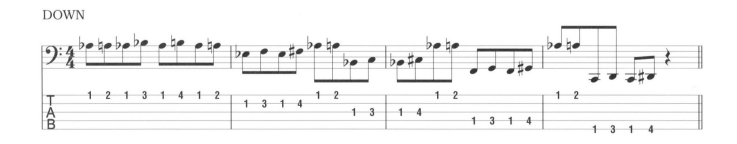

♩ = 60/180

UP

DOWN

UP

DOWN

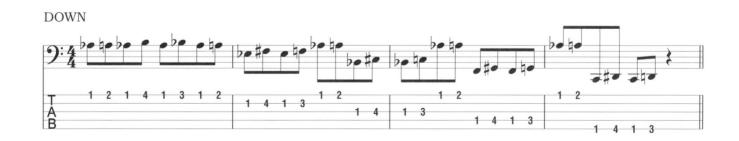

Part D

Finger independence exercises centered around finger 4 (upward motion)

♩ = 60/180

UP

DOWN

♩ = 60/180

UP

DOWN

♩ = 60/180

UP

DOWN

♩ = 60/180

UP

240

DOWN

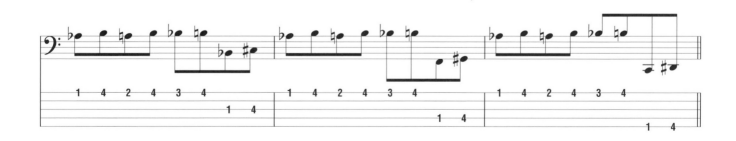

BASS RECORDED VERSIONS

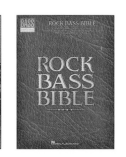

Bass Recorded Versions feature authentic transcriptions written in standard notation and tablature for bass guitar. This series features complete bass lines from the classics to contemporary superstars.

25 Essential Rock Bass Classics
00690210 / $19.99

Avenged Sevenfold – Nightmare
00691054 / $19.99

The Beatles – Abbey Road
00128336 / $24.99

The Beatles – 1962-1966
00690556 / $19.99

The Beatles – 1967-1970
00690557 / $24.99

Best of Bass Tab
00141806 / $17.99

The Best of Blink 182
00690549 / $18.99

Blues Bass Classics
00690291 / $22.99

Boston – Bass Collection
00690935 / $19.95

Stanley Clarke – Collection
00672307 / $22.99

Dream Theater – Bass Anthology
00119345 / $29.99

Funk Bass Bible
00690744 / $27.99

Hard Rock Bass Bible
00690746 / $22.99

**Jimi Hendrix –
Are You Experienced?**
00690371 / $17.95

Jimi Hendrix – Bass Tab Collection
00160505 / $24.99

Iron Maiden – Bass Anthology
00690867 / $24.99

Jazz Bass Classics
00102070 / $19.99

The Best of Kiss
00690080 / $22.99

**Lynyrd Skynyrd –
All-Time Greatest Hits**
00690956 / $24.99

Bob Marley – Bass Collection
00690568 / $24.99

Mastodon – Crack the Skye
00691007 / $19.99

Megadeth – Bass Anthology
00691191 / $22.99

Metal Bass Tabs
00103358 / $22.99

Best of Marcus Miller
00690811 / $29.99

Motown Bass Classics
00690253 / $19.99

Muse – Bass Tab Collection
00123275 / $22.99

Nirvana – Bass Collection
00690066 / $19.99

**Nothing More –
Guitar & Bass Collection**
00265439 / $24.99

The Offspring – Greatest Hits
00690809 / $17.95

The Essential Jaco Pastorius
00690420 / $22.99

**Jaco Pastorius –
Greatest Jazz Fusion Bass Player**
00690421 / $24.99

Pearl Jam – Ten
00694882 / $22.99

Pink Floyd – Dark Side of the Moon
00660172 / $19.99

The Best of Police
00660207 / $24.99

Pop/Rock Bass Bible
00690747 / $24.99

Queen – The Bass Collection
00690065 / $22.99

R&B Bass Bible
00690745 / $24.99

Rage Against the Machine
00690248 / $22.99

**Red Hot Chili Peppers –
BloodSugarSexMagik**
00690064 / $22.99

**Red Hot Chili Peppers –
By the Way**
00690585 / $24.99

**Red Hot Chili Peppers –
Californication**
00690390 / $22.99

**Red Hot Chili Peppers –
Greatest Hits**
00690675 / $22.99

**Red Hot Chili Peppers –
I'm with You**
00691167 / $22.99

**Red Hot Chili Peppers –
One Hot Minute**
00690091 / $22.99

**Red Hot Chili Peppers –
Stadium Arcadium**
00690853 / Book Only $24.95

Rock Bass Bible
00690446 / $22.99

Rolling Stones – Bass Collection
00690256 / $24.99

Royal Blood
00151826 / $24.99

**Rush – The Spirit of Radio:
Greatest Hits 1974-1987**
00323856 / $24.99

Best of Billy Sheehan
00173972 / $24.99

Slap Bass Bible
00159716 / $29.99

Sly & The Family Stone for Bass
00109733 / $24.99

Best of Yes
00103044 / $24.99

Best of ZZ Top for Bass
00691069 / $24.99

HAL•LEONARD®

Visit Hal Leonard Online at
www.halleonard.com

Prices, contents & availability subject to change without notice.
Some products may not be available outside the U.S.A.

HAL•LEONARD® BASS PLAY-ALONG

The Bass Play-Along™ Series will help you play your favorite songs quickly and easily! Just follow the tab, listen to the audio to hear how the bass should sound, and then play-along using the separate backing tracks. The melody and lyrics are also included in the book in case you want to sing, or to simply help you follow along. The audio files are enhanced so you can adjust the recording to any tempo without changing pitch!

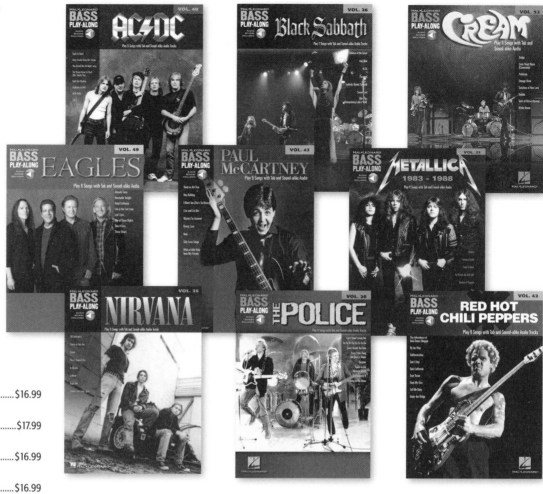

1. Rock
00699674 Book/Online Audio $16.99

2. R&B
00699675 Book/Online Audio $17.99

3. Songs for Beginners
00346426 Book/Online Audio $16.99

4. '90s Rock
00294992 Book/Online Audio $16.99

5. Funk
00699680 Book/Online Audio $17.99

6. Classic Rock
00699678 Book/Online Audio $17.99

9. Blues
00699817 Book•Online Audio $16.99

10. Jimi Hendrix – Smash Hits
00699815 Book/Online Audio $19.99

12. Punk Classics
00699814 Book/CD Pack $12.99

13. The Beatles
00275504 Book/Online Audio $17.99

14. Modern Rock
00699821 Book/CD Pack $14.99

15. Mainstream Rock
00699822 Book/CD Pack $14.99

16. '80s Metal
00699825 Book/CD Pack $16.99

17. Pop Metal
00699826 Book/CD Pack $14.99

18. Blues Rock
00699828 Book/CD Pack $19.99

19. Steely Dan
00700203 Book/Online Audio $17.99

20. The Police
00700270 Book/Online Audio $19.99

21. Metallica: 1983-1988
00234338 Book/Online Audio $19.99

22. Metallica: 1991-2016
00234339 Book/Online Audio $19.99

23. Pink Floyd – Dark Side of The Moon
00700847 Book/Online Audio $16.99

24. Weezer
00700960 Book/CD Pack $17.99

25. Nirvana
00701047 Book/Online Audio $17.99

26. Black Sabbath
00701180 Book/Online Audio $17.99

27. Kiss
00701181 Book/Online Audio $17.99

28. The Who
00701182 Book/Online Audio $19.99

29. Eric Clapton
00701183 Book/Online Audio $17.99

30. Early Rock
00701184 Book/CD Pack $15.99

31. The 1970s
00701185 Book/CD Pack $14.99

32. Cover Band Hits
00211598 Book/Online Audio $16.99

34. Easy Songs
00701480 Book/Online Audio $17.99

35. Bob Marley
00701702 Book/Online Audio $19.99

36. Aerosmith
00701886 Book/CD Pack $14.99

37. Modern Worship
00701920 Book/Online Audio $19.99

38. Avenged Sevenfold
00702386 Book/CD Pack $16.99

39. Queen
00702387 Book/Online Audio $17.99

40. AC/DC
14041594 Book/Online Audio $17.99

41. U2
00702582 Book/Online Audio $19.99

42. Red Hot Chili Peppers
00702991 Book/Online Audio $22.99

43. Paul McCartney
00703079 Book/Online Audio $19.99

44. Megadeth
00703080 Book/CD Pack $16.99

46. Best Bass Lines Ever
00103359 Book/Online Audio $19.99

47. Dream Theater
00111940 Book/Online Audio $24.99

48. James Brown
00117421 Book/CD Pack $16.99

49. Eagles
00119936 Book/Online Audio $19.99

50. Jaco Pastorius
00128407 Book/Online Audio $19.99

51. Stevie Ray Vaughan
00146154 Book/CD Pack $16.99

52. Cream
00146159 Book/Online Audio $19.99

56. Bob Seger
00275503 Book/Online Audio $16.99

57. Iron Maiden
00278398 Book/Online Audio $19.99

58. Southern Rock
00278436 Book/Online Audio $17.99

Visit Hal Leonard Online at **www.halleonard.com**

Prices, contents, and availability subject to change without notice.

BASS BUILDERS

A series of technique book/audio packages created for the purposeful building and development of your chops. Each volume is written by an expert in that particular technique. And with the inclusion of audio, the added dimension of hearing exactly how to play particular grooves and techniques make these truly like private lessons.

BASS GROOVES
by Jon Liebman
00696028 Book/Online Audio $22.99

BASS IMPROVISATION
by Ed Friedland
00695164 Book/Online Audio $19.99

BLUES BASS
by Jon Liebman
00695235 Book/Online Audio $22.99

BUILDING WALKING BASS LINES
by Ed Friedland
00695008 Book/Online Audio $22.99

RON CARTER –
BUILDING JAZZ BASS LINES
00841240 Book/Online Audio $22.99

DICTIONARY OF BASS GROOVES
by Sean Malone
00695266 Book/Online Audio $16.99

EXPANDING WALKING BASS LINES
by Ed Friedland
00695026 Book/Online Audio $22.99

FINGERBOARD HARMONY FOR BASS
by Gary Willis
00695043 Book/Online Audio $19.99

FUNK BASS
by Jon Liebman
00699348 Book/Online Audio $22.99

FUNK/FUSION BASS
by Jon Liebman
00696553 Book/Online Audio $24.99

HIP-HOP BASS
by Josquin des Prés
00695589 Book/Online Audio $15.99

JAZZ BASS
by Ed Friedland
00695084 Book/Online Audio $17.99

JERRY JEMMOTT –
BLUES AND RHYTHM &
BLUES BASS TECHNIQUE
00695176 Book/CD Pack.. $24.99

JUMP 'N' BLUES BASS
by Keith Rosier
00695292 Book/Online Audio $17.99

THE LOST ART OF COUNTRY BASS
by Keith Rosier
00695107 Book/Online Audio $22.99

PENTATONIC SCALES FOR BASS
by Ed Friedland
00696224 Book/Online Audio $22.99

REGGAE BASS
by Ed Friedland
00695163 Book/Online Audio $17.99

'70S FUNK & DISCO BASS
by Josquin des Prés
00695614 Book/Online Audio $19.99

SIMPLIFIED SIGHT-READING FOR BASS
by Josquin des Prés
00695085 Book/Online Audio $17.99

6-STRING BASSICS
by David Gross
00695221 Book/Online Audio $16.99

HAL•LEONARD®

halleonard.com

Prices, contents and availability subject to change without notice; All prices are listed in U.S. funds